THE ELEMENTS

# Titanium

Chris Woodford

BENCHMARK BOOKS

Benchmark Books
Marshall Cavendish
99 White Plains Road
Tarrytown, New York 10591
www.marshallcavendish.com



Library of Congress Cataloging-in-Publication Data

Woodford, Chris, 1943–.
Titanium / by Chris Woodford.
p. cm. — (The elements)
Includes index.
Summary: Explores the history of titanium and
explains its chemistry, its uses, and
its importance in our lives.
ISBN 0-7614-1461-4
1. Titanium—Juvenile literature. [1. Titanium.] I. Title.
II. Elements (Benchmark Books)
QD181.T6 W66 2003
546'.512—dc21 2001008743

Printed in Hong Kong

**Picture credits**

Front cover: NASA
Back cover: Pictor International
DePuy: (S-ROM is a registered trademark of Johnson & Johnson Ltd.) 21 (*above right*), 21 (*below left*)
DOE Albany Research Center: 8 (*below left*)
HEAD Sport AG: 23
Image Bank: Jeff Hunter *i*, 27; Steve Allen 14
NASA: 19
NewsCast: British Airways plc 18
NOAA: OAR/NURP; Harbor Branch Oceanographic Institute 26
Pains Fireworks Ltd.: 5
Pictor International: 15, 24
Rolls-Royce plc: 10
Science & Society Picture Library: Bousfield/BKK *iii*, 16; Science Museum 20
Science Photo Library: Jerry Mason 12; Klaus Guldbrandsen 11; TEK Image 8 (*above right*)
Still Pictures: Jonathan Kaplan 7
Titanium International Ltd.: 4
© Titanium Metals Corporation: 22, 30
TRH Pictures: Toyota 25
US DoD: 17

Series created by Brown Partworks Ltd.
Designed by Sarah Williams

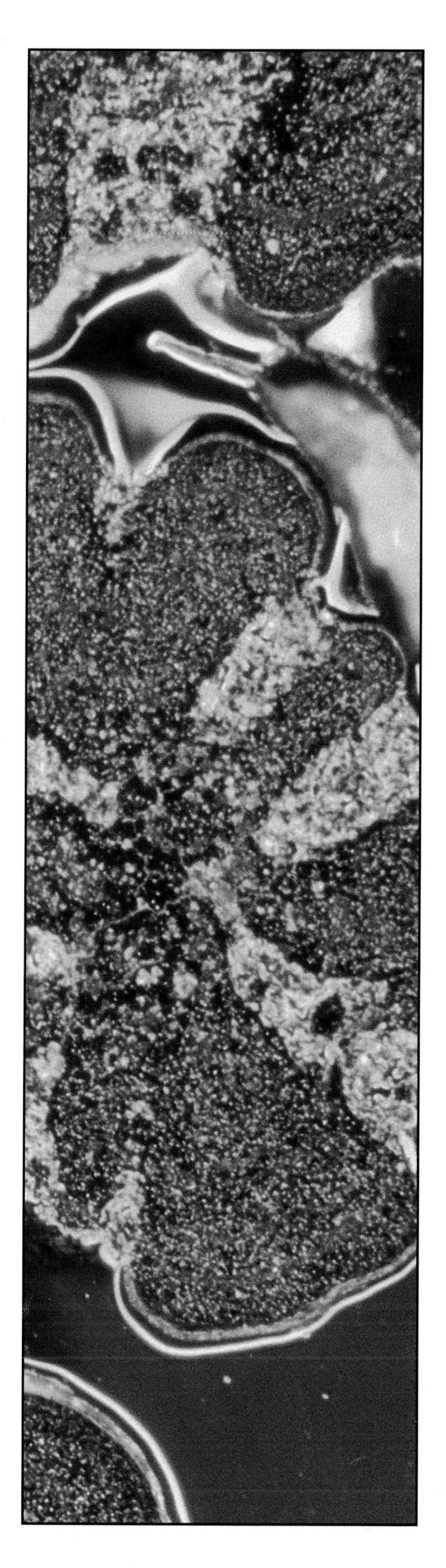

# Contents

# What is titanium?

Titanium is a strong, light metal with the chemical symbol Ti. The name *titanium* comes from the Greek *Titans.* These mythological giants were noted for their strength, and titanium certainly lives up to this description. Metallic titanium is most often used to make structural parts for airplanes and their engines. Titanium and its compounds also make paints that are whiter, wetsuits that are warmer, and eyeglass frames that are lighter.

DID YOU KNOW?

***TRANSITION ELEMENTS***

Titanium is in the fourth horizontal row, or period, of the periodic table of chemical elements. It is grouped with a number of other elements called transition metals. Other transition metals include copper, gold, iron, platinum, and zinc.

Most chemical elements react with other chemical elements by losing, gaining, or sharing electrons from their outer electron shells. When transition metals react, electrons in their inner, neighboring electron shell can also be involved. This makes the chemistry of the transition metals very unusual. It is very different from the chemistry of other elements in the periodic table.

## The titanium atom

Everything you see around you consists of microscopic particles called atoms. Some ancient Greek philosophers were the first to propose that atoms were the smallest particles of matter that could exist. Indeed, the word *atom* comes from the Greek word *atomos,* which means "cannot be divided."

We now know that atoms contain even smaller particles—protons, neutrons, and electrons. The protons and neutrons are found in the tiny nucleus at the center of each atom. The electrons revolve around the nucleus in a series of layers called electron shells.

*Pure titanium, cast into a variety of different shapes, has a silvery gray color. This color comes from a thin layer of titanium dioxide ($TiO_2$) formed at the surface when the metal reacts with oxygen in the air.*

*Fireworks often contain titanium compounds. They make the explosions bright and white.*

## Making molecules

An atom is stable if its outer electron shell is full. Atoms transfer and share electrons with other atoms so that they all end up with complete shells. As the electrons move, they form bonds between the atoms, resulting in molecules and compounds.

Each atom of titanium has 22 positively charged protons in the nucleus. No other chemical element has this number of protons, so titanium is said to have an atomic number of 22.

Neutrons are about the same size as protons but have no electrical charge. Most titanium atoms contain 26 neutrons. The total number of protons and neutrons in an atom is known as the atomic mass. Titanium has an atomic mass of 48 (22 protons plus 26 neutrons).

For every titanium atom, the number of protons and electrons is equal. This means that titanium has 22 negatively charged electrons revolving around the nucleus. Titanium has a very unusual arrangement of electrons compared to most other chemical elements.

TITANIUM ATOM

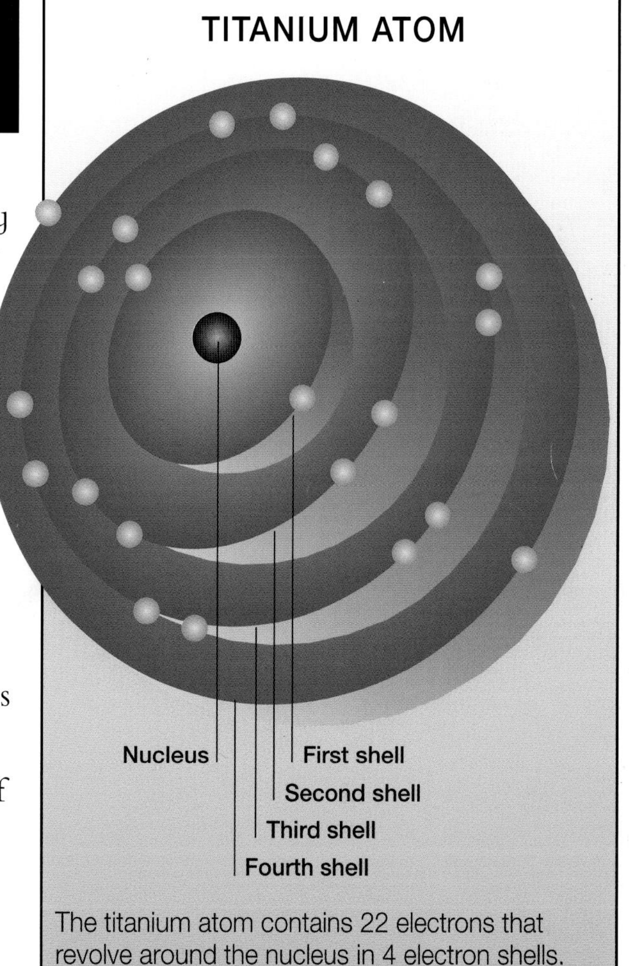


The titanium atom contains 22 electrons that revolve around the nucleus in 4 electron shells. There are 2 electrons in the first shell, 8 electrons in the second shell, 10 electrons in the third shell, and 2 electrons in the outer shell.

# Where is it found?

The next time you go to a sandy beach, take a close look at the sand. The tiny black particles you will see contain titanium. This metal is also found in rocks, soil, and deposits deep under the sea. In fact, titanium is the fourth most common metal on Earth, after aluminum, iron, and magnesium.

DID YOU KNOW?

***TITANIUM IN SPACE***

Titanium is thought to have formed and then scattered by nuclear reactions that occur in exploding stars called supernovas. Space probes have discovered titanium on the Moon, in asteroids, and in meteorites. Astronomers have also found that a star called Cassiopeia A (Cas A for short) contains large amounts of a radioactive form of titanium called titanium-44. It seems fitting that the titanium from which rockets and satellites are built originally came from space.

## Titanium in the ground

Titanium does not occur as a pure metal in nature. It forms compounds called ores with other chemical elements. The two most common titanium ores are rutile and ilmenite. The black particles found in sand are made of rutile. This ore consists of a compound called titanium dioxide ($TiO_2$), along with traces of other elements.

Ilmenite is made up of a compound containing iron, titanium, and oxygen ($FeTiO_3$). Ilmenite takes its name from the Ilmen Range of the Ural Mountains in Russia, where it is found in large quantities. Many other countries produce pure titanium from rutile and ilmenite. They include Australia, Brazil, Canada, Norway, and the United States.

*Rutile is often embedded in crystals of quartz, making them a brownish-yellow color.*

# How was it discovered?

Many people think titanium is a modern and high-tech material. It is true that titanium has been widely used since the 1950s, but it was first discovered more than 200 years ago. In 1791, English clergyman and chemist William Gregor (1761–1817) found a sample of black sand at the beach in Menaccan in Cornwall, England. Gregor analyzed the sample and identified a reddish-brown compound, now known to be titanium dioxide. Gregor called the new substance menacchanine after the town where it was found.

Five years later, German chemist Martin Heinrich Klaproth (1743–1817) discovered the same material in rocks he found in Hungary. Klaproth realized that the substance was a metal oxide—a compound containing a metal combined with one or more oxygen atoms. Klaproth named the new metal titanium.

## DID YOU KNOW?

***PURE TITANIUM***

Although both William Gregor and Martin Heinrich Klaproth extracted titanium dioxide from sand and rock samples, neither could isolate pure titanium. It would be another 120 years before titanium was first extracted in a laboratory. In 1910, U.S. chemist Matthew Hunter and his colleagues reacted titanium tetrachloride ($TiCl_4$) with sodium metal to produce pure titanium metal and sodium chloride (NaCl). This reaction forms the basis of the modern method for making pure titanium metal—the Kroll process.

*A villager from Madagascar holds a handful of sand containing the black mineral titanium dioxide. Today, most titanium metal produced in industry is extracted from titanium dioxide.*

# Where does titanium come from?

Titanium has many applications in modern science and engineering. As a result, it has become increasingly necessary to extract more titanium from its ores. In 1910, U.S. chemist Matthew Hunter isolated titanium in the laboratory by reacting titanium tetrachloride ($TiCl_4$) with sodium. In 1937, German chemist William A. Kroll extended Hunter's technique. Kroll's method continues to be the main commercial method of isolating pure titanium from its ores.

*Two foundry workers pour molten titanium into an ingot mold. The clothes of the workers are silvered to reflect the intense heat of the molten metal.*

## The Kroll process

The first step in the Kroll process is to react the titanium dioxide ($TiO_2$) in the ore with chlorine ($Cl_2$). This reaction produces a light yellow liquid called titanium tetrachloride. This liquid passes into a large stainless steel or carbon vessel containing molten (liquid) magnesium metal.

Inside the vessel, the molten magnesium strips chlorine atoms from the titanium tetrachloride to produce magnesium chloride ($MgCl_2$) and pure titanium metal

*William A. Kroll shown here with his equipment for making metallic titanium. Kroll's process has also been adapted for the production of pure zirconium.*

## ATOMS AT WORK

An industrial chemical reaction called the Kroll process is used to produce pure titanium metal. In this reaction, a substance called titanium tetrachloride reacts with magnesium metal. Titanium tetrachloride consists of one atom of titanium joined to four atoms of chlorine.

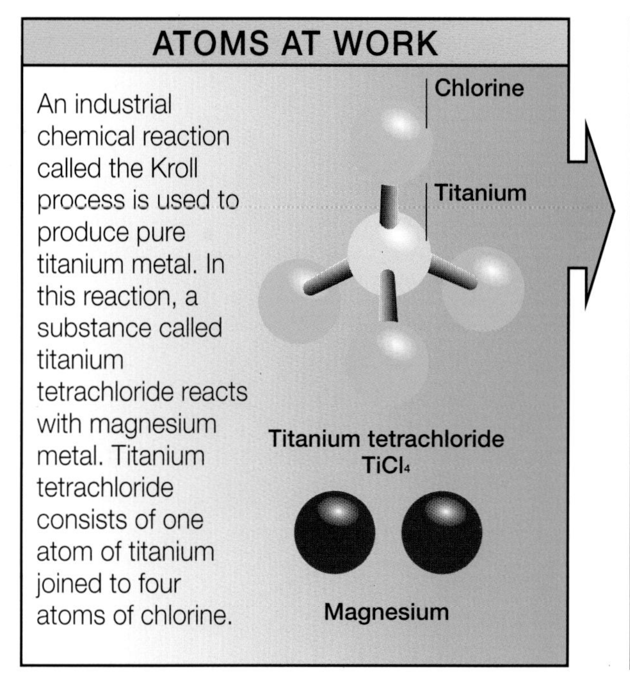


In the first stage of the Kroll process, titanium tetrachloride and magnesium are heated to 1800° F (1000° C). The extremely high temperature breaks the chemical bonds between the titanium atom and the four chlorine atoms to leave pure titanium metal.

The four chlorine atoms are free to form new bonds. The chlorine atoms react with the magnesium atoms to make magnesium chloride. Two chlorine atoms join to one magnesium atom to produce a molecule of magnesium chloride. The titanium atom is left on its own.

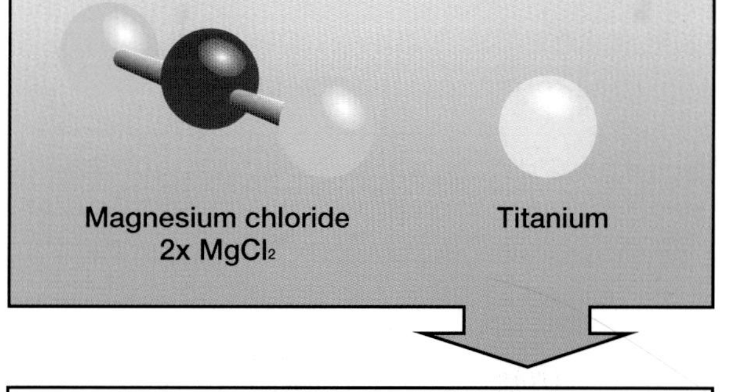


The chemical reaction that takes place in the Kroll process can be written like this:

$$2Mg + TiCl_4 \rightarrow Ti + 2MgCl_2$$

This equation tells us that two atoms of magnesium react with one molecule of titanium tetrachloride to form one atom of titanium and two molecules of magnesium chloride.

in the form of a sponge. This reaction takes place in an atmosphere of argon gas, which does not interfere with the reaction. If the vessel were filled with air, gases in the air would react with the titanium sponge and spoil the finished product.

The titanium sponge contains gaps that fill up with molecules of the magnesium chloride. In much the same way as you would squeeze out a sponge to remove water, the Kroll process involves compressing the titanium sponge to remove the magnesium chloride.

The titanium sponge is then purified using acids or distillation (separating chemicals by heating them to different temperatures). The purified titanium is then melted down into blocks of pure metal called ingots.

*Titanium is very strong, light, and can withstand extremely high temperatures. These properties make the metal ideal for use in the construction of some components of this Rolls Royce airplane engine.*

# Special characteristics

Titanium has many desirable physical properties. The pure metal is relatively soft and weak, but titanium becomes much stronger when it is mixed with other metals to form alloys. Titanium also reacts very easily with oxygen. In the presence of air, titanium metal becomes coated with a layer of titanium dioxide. This oxide layer helps to resist corrosion from salt water and other chemicals. The high melting point of titanium (3035° F or 1668° C) also means it is an ideal material for the construction of high-speed aircraft and space vehicles.

**DID YOU KNOW?**

***ISOTOPES***

Most chemical elements occur in different forms called isotopes. The isotopes of titanium all have 22 protons in the nucleus, but each one has a different number of neutrons in the nucleus. The most common titanium isotope is titanium-48, which has 22 protons and 26 neutrons. (The number 48 tells us the atomic mass is 22 protons plus 26 neutrons, which equals 48.) Other common isotopes are titanium-46 (24 neutrons), titanium-47 (25 neutrons), titanium-49 (27 neutrons), and titanium-50 (28 neutrons).

# How titanium reacts

Titanium may react in different ways with the same element. For example, titanium forms three different oxides.

## Titanium and its oxides

If one titanium atom reacts with two oxygen atoms, the titanium donates four electrons to the oxygen atoms. Since four electrons are involved, titanium is said to have a valency of four in this reaction. The resulting compound is called titanium (IV) oxide ($TiO_2$), or titanium dioxide.

However, two titanium atoms can also react with three oxygen atoms to form titanium (III) oxide ($Ti_2O_3$) or dititanium trioxide. Here, each titanium atom donates three electrons to the oxygen atoms, so titanium is said to have a valency of three.

One titanium atom can also react with one oxygen atom to form a compound called titanium (II) oxide (TiO) or titanium monoxide. In this case, the titanium atom has a valency of two,

*An electric arc furnace is used to produce an alloy of titanium and nickel. A massive electric current passes through the metals. The current acts like a lightning bolt, heating the metals to their melting points.*

*Huge bags of titanium (IV) oxide (titanium dioxide) powder are stored in a warehouse in the United States. This compound is one of three oxides of titanium. It is a very important pigment used in the paint, paper, and plastic industries.*

because it donates two electrons to the oxygen atom. Since titanium has three different valencies (two, three, and four), it is described as having multiple valencies.

## Other titanium reactions

Titanium reacts with many different chemical elements. For example, titanium forms halides with halogens such as chlorine and fluorine. Titanium halides include titanium tetrachloride ($TiCl_4$) and titanium tetrafluoride ($TiF_4$). Titanium also reacts with hydrogen to form titanium hydride ($TiH_2$), with carbon to form titanium carbide (TiC), and with hydrogen sulfide gas to form titanium sulfide ($TiS_2$). Titanium is virtually unique among all the chemical elements, because the powdered metal burns in nitrogen gas to form titanium nitride (TiN). This reaction occurs during the bright explosions of fireworks.

## Titanium catalysts

Some elements or compounds make chemical reactions occur more quickly or easily. Chemists call these compounds catalysts. Many titanium compounds are used to speed up chemical reactions in industrial processes. For example, a complex compound made up of titanium, aluminum, carbon, chlorine, and hydrogen atoms is used as an industrial catalyst to make a plastic called polyethylene. Similarly, titanium trichloride ($TiCl_3$) is another industrial catalyst used to make a plastic called polypropylene.

## Making alloys

As a pure metal, titanium is a strong, lightweight, and heat-resistant element. It also reacts with many other substances to form titanium compounds. Titanium can be combined with other metals to make substances called alloys. An alloy is a mixture of two or more metals that combines the best properties of each metal. Alloys containing titanium have different physical and chemical properties than pure titanium. In the aerospace industry, for example, titanium is often mixed with metals such as aluminum, tin, vanadium, and zirconium to make alloys that are stronger, tougher, and more durable. These alloys can also work at high temperatures and resist corrosion from substances in the air, such as water and oxygen.

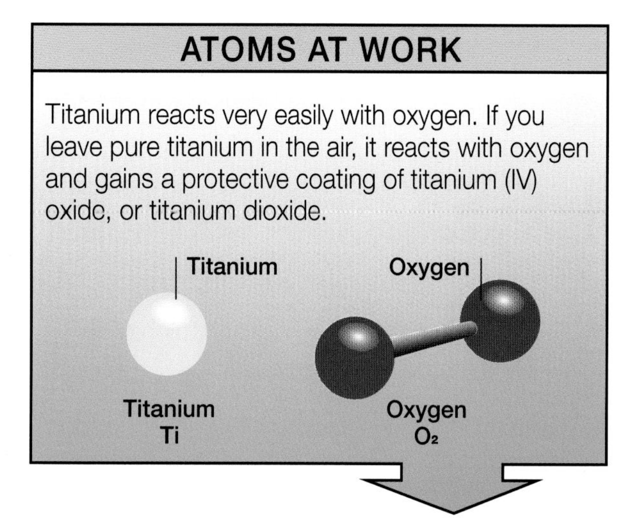


In the most common reaction between titanium and oxygen gas, one atom of titanium reacts with a molecule of oxygen gas. The chemical bonds between the two oxygen atoms break. The oxygen atoms are then free to form new bonds with the titanium atom.

During the reaction, the titanium atom donates some of its electrons to the oxygen atoms. Each oxygen atom gains two electrons when they bond to the titanium atom. One molecule of titanium dioxide (a pure white powder) forms.

**Titanium (IV) oxide, or titanium dioxide**
**$TiO_2$**

The chemical reaction that takes place can be written like this:

$$Ti + O_2 \rightarrow TiO_2$$

The number of atoms on each side of the equation is the same, although the atoms are in new combinations.

# Brilliant white

Different objects get their color from the way they reflect different colors of light. Tomatoes reflect mainly red light, while green apples reflect mainly green light. Titanium dioxide ($TiO_2$) powder is a brilliant white color because it reflects almost all the different colors of light. In fact, titanium dioxide is better at reflecting light than almost any other substance. This makes titanium dioxide powder a very useful pigment—a chemical that gives an object color—in substances like paints. In fact, around 95 percent of all titanium used in industry is in the form of titanium dioxide pigment.

Since titanium dioxide reflects light so well, it is virtually opaque. Light does not pass through opaque objects, so paints that contain titanium dioxide cover surfaces very well. This property also makes titanium dioxide useful for disguising flaws in materials like plastics.

*The titanium dioxide in white paint is an extremely stable substance, because it does not react with other substances in the air. As a result, white paints will not discolor as they get older.*

## DID YOU KNOW?

### *STOPPING SUNBURN*

Sunscreens and sunblocks work by either absorbing (soaking up) or reflecting (bouncing back) harmful ultraviolet radiation emitted by the Sun. This helps to protect the skin from aging too quickly and also reduces the risk of dangerous diseases like skin cancer.

When you rub sunscreen onto your face, the fine white coating that you see is probably titanium dioxide. Although other chemicals can be used, titanium dioxide is preferred because it does not irritate the skin and is safer to use. Some sunscreens contain fine particles of titanium dioxide, called microtitanium dioxide. These particles cover the skin much more effectively and provide greater protection than normal sunscreens and sunblocks.

Finally, titanium dioxide powder is nontoxic, which means it is not harmful to humans or other animals. In the past, toxic chemicals, like lead carbonate, were added to paints to make them white. Paints containing titanium dioxide are safe to use for most applications. Properties such as these make titanium dioxide the most common white pigment used in industry today, not just in dyes, paints, and plastics, but also in ceramics, cosmetics, glassware, inks, paper, rubber, and even toothpaste.

*A Japanese geisha (female entertainer) wears cosmetic face-powder containing titanium dioxide.*

## Ultraviolet protection

Many plastics are said to "age" with time because a component of sunlight, called ultraviolet light, breaks them down. Scientists now add titanium dioxide to plastics to soak up ultraviolet light. Polyvinylchloride (PVC) window frames now contain titanium dioxide to prevent the damage from ultraviolet light.

## Making titanium dioxide

Titanium dioxide consists of tiny particles called crystals. Producing titanium dioxide crystals for use in pigments is an exact science. Each crystal must measure between 0.2 and 0.4 micrometers (one micrometer is one millionth of a meter). If the crystals are even slightly imperfect, they will reflect light poorly and lose their bright white color. Each stage of the process involves careful monitoring and quality control. Instruments such as spectrophotometers and colorimeters are used to check that the crystals reflect light in exactly the right way.

*Only the purest crystals of $TiO_2$ with exactly the right size, structure, and shape are used to produce brilliant white titanium dioxide for the paint and printing industry.*

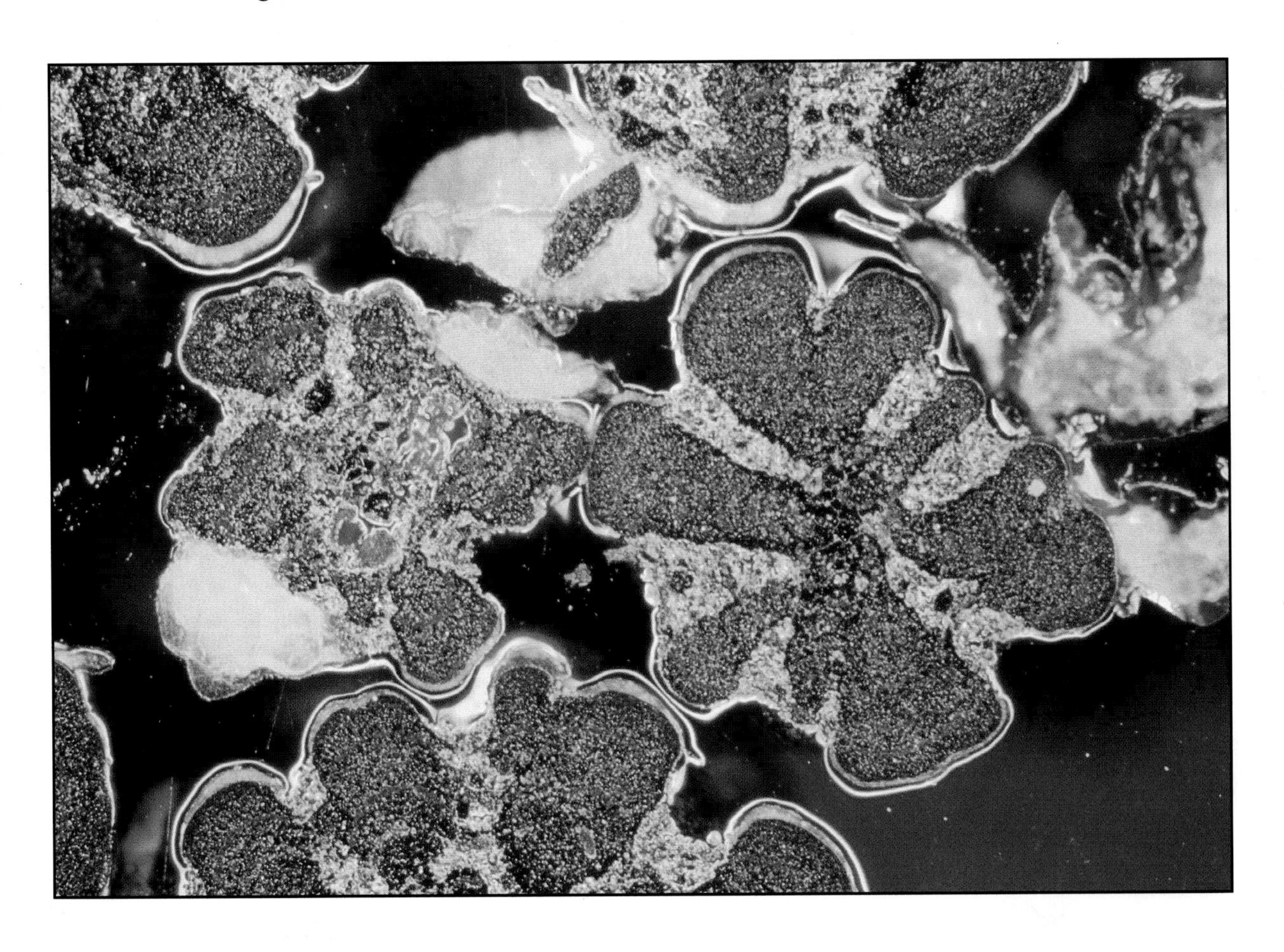

# Titanium in the air and space

If you held a piece of titanium in one hand and a similar-sized piece of steel in the other, you would notice that the titanium weighs much less than the steel. As well as being much lighter than steel, titanium is also stronger. If you built two identical airplanes, one from titanium and one from steel, the titanium plane would be half the weight of the steel plane, but much stronger. The titanium plane would fly faster and use much less fuel.

Once the world's fastest and highest-flying airplane, the United States Air Force (USAF) SR71 Blackbird (now out of service), was built entirely from titanium for just this reason. Military airplanes contain more titanium than commercial airliners, because they have to work in more demanding environments. Although titanium is much more expensive than steel, the military can afford to spend more money on high-tech materials.

It is not just strength and lightness that make titanium so useful in aerospace construction. Titanium alloys remain strong at very high temperatures (up to about 1100° F or 600° C), so they are used to make the working parts of airplane jet engines. Unlike steel, titanium alloys are resistant to corrosion (they do not rust). Engineers have also found that they need to use less titanium than steel to make identical engine parts.

*Each USAF B2 Stealth bomber contains more than 100 tons (91 tonnes) of titanium and titanium alloys.*

## DID YOU KNOW?

### *THE CONCORDE*

The Concorde is the world's only supersonic passenger airplane. Developed by aviation engineers in Britain and France, it can cruise at Mach 2, which is twice the speed of sound (more than 1,350 mph, or 2,170 km/h). Engineers originally planned to build the main structure of the aircraft using titanium alloys. But this plan was too expensive. Aluminum alloys were used instead, but the aircraft's landing gear and some of the engine parts were made out of titanium and steel.

If titanium helped to get the Concorde into the air, it also played a crucial part in grounding the entire fleet. In July 2000, a disastrous crash in Paris, France, killed 113 people. During takeoff, the airplane ran over a piece of titanium on the runway. The titanium had fallen from the engine of another aircraft. Any other metal might simply have been squashed by the weight of an airplane, but the titanium was so strong that it caused one of the airplane's tires to explode. Aviation authorities immediately grounded the entire fleet of airplanes. The service only resumed in November 2001, when a number of safety regulations were put into place to prevent a similar disaster from happening again.

*The Concorde made its first flight in 1969 and entered commercial service seven years later. It cost the French and British governments over $2.8 billion.*

Titanium alloys can be worked into many different shapes and sizes. These alloys are also very reliable. They are much less likely to fail through metal fatigue—the gradual weakening of a metal during repeated use—than steel. This is extremely important in airplane construction, because fatigue has caused a number of crashes.

*The Mercury and Apollo spacecraft that took part in NASA's missions to the Moon were built using titanium frameworks covered with steel.*

DID YOU KNOW?

***TITANIUM TO THE MOON***

If NASA (the National Aeronautics and Space Administration) had not commenced its space program in the late 1950s, titanium alloys would not have been developed so quickly for use in military and commercial airplanes. Components made from titanium were an obvious choice for the NASA missions to the Moon because of their low weights and their immense strength at high temperatures. It seems fitting that rocks collected during the *Apollo 17* mission led to the discovery of the existence of titanium on the Moon.

# Titanium in medicine

The human body is made of some remarkable materials, all of which are designed to work continuously for many years. Over time or with disease, however, limbs or organs may become damaged beyond repair. A branch of medicine called biomedical engineering has enabled people to design and make artificial body parts to replace those that are damaged or worn out. One of the main problems for biomedical engineers has been to find suitable materials to make these artificial body parts. Strength, lightness, and resistance to saltwater, acids, and other body fluids make titanium an ideal choice for this purpose. Titanium parts continue to work for many years without rusting or wearing out. Many medical items now have components made from titanium alloys, including artificial hip joints, eyeglass frames, and dentures. Doctors have even developed an artificial heart made from titanium.

## Dental implants

When teeth decay, they are usually replaced with dentures—false teeth mounted on a plastic support. A modern dental technique involves replacing lost or damaged teeth with implants made from titanium. This process has two main stages. The first is a surgical procedure in which the titanium implant is fixed to the jawbone. About six months later, when the implant is secure, a false tooth is permanently attached to the implant. Unlike traditional dentures, titanium implants stay in place forever.

*Artificial hearts made from titanium and plastic might be available for human transplantation by 2005.*

DID YOU KNOW?

***IN A SPIN***

Some of the equipment used in medicine is also made from titanium. An ultracentrifuge is a device that separates solids from liquids in tubes arranged like helicopter rotors. The rotors of an ultracentrifuge spin at very high speeds. As the mixture spins, forces up to one million times that of gravity pull heavy materials to the bottom of the tubes. Lighter materials stay at the top. The rotors of most ultracentrifuges are made of titanium, which is both light enough to spin around quickly and strong enough to withstand the tremendous forces.

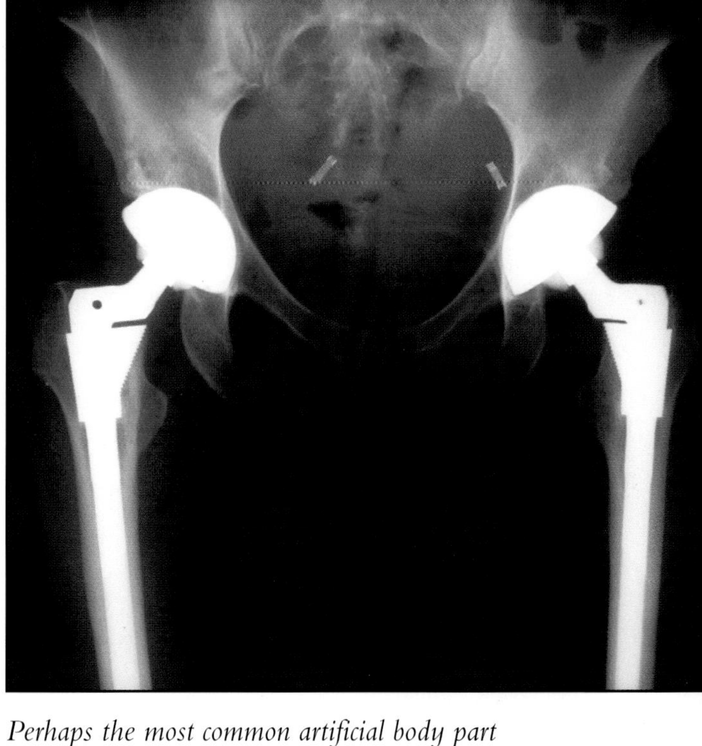

*Perhaps the most common artificial body part today is the titanium ball-and-socket joint used to replace a hip joint damaged by arthritis (left). The X-ray image shown above shows two titanium joints in place following surgery.*

## Alloy with a memory

Nitinol—an alloy of nickel and titanium—is widely used in medicine. It is used in hip-joint replacements and stents—metal braces that strengthen blood vessels from the inside. Nitinol is popular because it can be folded up or bent but will later return to its original shape. Scientists think that the atoms in the alloy "remember" their original positions. Even if the nitinol is folded into a completely different shape, the atoms will always revert back to the original arrangement.

# Titanium at work

Titanium and its alloys have found many different uses in the world around us. Their light weight and strength make them the material of choice in high-tech sporting equipment. U.S. golfing champion Tiger Woods uses titanium golf clubs. Titanium alloys have also replaced aluminum and steel in the manufacturing of bicycle frames. Titanium alloys are lighter, stiffer, and hold their shape better over time than other metals and alloys.

Titanium also has many applications in the home. Kitchen knives made from titanium stay sharper longer than stainless steel blades. These titanium items do not taint foods in the same way as some other metals and plastics. Titanium has also been used on nonstick cookware such as frying pans. Forty times harder than stainless steel, titanium does not scratch like nonstick Teflon (another product of the space age), so it lasts much longer.

*The exterior of the Guggenheim Museum in Bilbao, Spain, is coated with a thin layer of titanium.*

*U.S. tennis champion Andre Agassi (1970– ) uses a tennis racket made from an alloy of titanium.*

> **DID YOU KNOW?**
>
> ***TITANIUM STRUCTURES***
>
> Titanium often plays an invisible role in making buildings stronger. Originally built in the 5th century B.C.E., the Parthenon on the Acropolis of Athens, Greece, has been reconstructed using titanium rods, which have strengthened the structure's original foundations. In more modern buildings, titanium plays a hidden role in the roof structures, window frames, and ventilators.
>
> In one building at least, titanium is much more apparent. When U.S. architect Frank Gehry (1929– ) designed the dazzling Guggenheim Museum in Bilbao, Spain, he chose to cover it with a thin layer of titanium. Patterned like fish scales, the titanium covering is expected to last at least 100 years. Apart from giving the building a striking appearance, the titanium scales will reflect heat away from the building, protecting the priceless collection of artwork inside.

## Titanium for show

Objects made from titanium look very attractive. Many items of jewelry, such as rings and watches, are now made from titanium. Titanium jewelry is decorated in a wide range of colors using special heat-treatment processes. The same processes are used to decorate eyeglass frames made from the nickel-titanium alloy nitinol. Although nitinol eyeglass frames are slightly more expensive than normal eyeglass frames, they are very flexible. They can be virtually bent in half and will return to their original shape. Decoratively finished titanium also gives a high-tech appearance to the design of personal computers. For example, the Titanium PowerBook G4 laptop computer, made by Apple Computers, is encased in pure titanium.

# Titanium in industry

*Parts of the machinery in breweries are often made from titanium and its alloys, because these materials are resistant to corrosive chemicals.*

Just as titanium and its alloys have revolutionized many consumer products, they have proved equally useful in a range of heavy-duty industrial applications. One of the most important properties of titanium is its ability to operate in very harsh environments. Unlike steel, which can rust or fatigue, titanium can withstand a wide range of corrosive chemicals, such as acids and saltwater. Despite its higher cost, titanium has replaced the use of metals like stainless steel in industries such as brewing, food production, papermaking, and petrochemicals.

In many hot countries water supplies are scarce. Factories called desalination plants are often used to remove the salt from seawater, making it safe to drink. The machinery in desalination plants is often made from titanium and its alloys. Saltwater corrodes stainless steel but does not destroy titanium, so the desalination plant will work longer.

Titanium is also good at withstanding the effects of other chemicals. To prevent pollution, many countries enforce tough environmental regulations. These laws

DID YOU KNOW?

***STORING NUCLEAR WASTE***

Nuclear power is a vital source of energy, but one of its biggest disadvantages is the deadly waste products generated as a result of the nuclear reactions. Harmful substances, such as plutonium and cesium, remain dangerously radioactive for thousands of years. As a result, engineers continue to look for ways to store nuclear waste safely.

Titanium silicates offer a solution to this problem. Titanium silicates contain titanium, silicon, and oxygen atoms bonded in a crystal structure. The titanium silicate crystals act like a sponge with large open spaces between the atoms. Most titanium silicates also contain sodium ions—an atom of sodium that is missing one electron—in the gaps. When radioactive cesium ions come into contact with titanium silicate crystals, the cesium ions try to replace the sodium ions and become trapped inside the crystal structure. Once the cesium waste has been locked away in the titanium silicate crystals, the crystals are stored in steel drums and buried deep underground.

force many industrial plants to clean their flue gases (smokestack emissions). Titanium and its alloys are often used to make the equipment that removes sulfur pollutants from flue gases. If other metals were used, the sulfur compounds would corrode them over time.

## The automobile industry

Many other industries have taken advantage of the properties of titanium and its alloys. The automobile industry is a good example. Many automobile engine parts are made from titanium, because they need to work continuously at high speeds and high temperatures. Most suspension springs are made from titanium because it is much lighter than steel and twice as flexible. Titanium's ability to withstand high temperatures also makes it an increasingly popular choice in vehicle exhaust systems. One day, it may even be possible to buy an automobile made entirely from titanium.

*The engine valves of many modern automobiles are now made from titanium.*

# Titanium at sea

Unlike most metals, titanium and its alloys are extremely resistant to the corrosive effect of saltwater. Today, titanium is a very useful material for many marine applications, including the pipes that support offshore oil rigs, submarine hulls, and ship propellers. Since titanium does not react with saltwater, the metal will not produce toxic chemicals that are harmful to fish and other marine life.

*The underwater cameras attached to this submersible are encased in a layer of titanium to protect the components from the damaging effects of saltwater.*

DID YOU KNOW?

***WARMER WETSUITS***

Seawater draws heat away from the human body about 25 times more quickly than air at the same temperature. That is why it often seems cold when you go swimming in the sea even on a hot day. Neoprene wetsuits made from synthetic rubber have revolutionized sports such as diving and surfing. The wetsuit traps a layer of warm air around the body, which helps people to stay warm in the water. The latest wetsuits are lined with a thin, flexible layer of titanium that reflects body heat back inside the suit. This insulates the body for longer periods of time and enables people to swim in the sea on colder days.

## Titanium propellers

Even metals that are fairly resistant to the corrosive effects of saltwater are damaged by the buffeting of the waves. When a propeller spins in the sea, it heats the water around it, creating bubbles that eat away at the metal from which it is made. This effect is called cavitation, and it can drastically shorten the life of propellers made from metals like steel. Titanium can withstand the effect of cavitation much better than most other metals. Many ship propellers are now made from titanium.

## Under pressure

Military submarines are designed to stay submerged for up to three years without resurfacing. Remaining underwater for such a long time places great demands on the materials from which they are made. The gradual corrosion and failure of the hull of a submarine would have a catastrophic effect. This problem is made worse by the pressure of the water pressing on the hull of the submarine, because water pressure increases with increasing depth.

In Russia, titanium is used to make the hulls and other parts of high-performance military submarines. The titanium submarines can dive deeper, move faster, and stay submerged for longer with less risk of failure. However, these titanium submarines are not perfect. In 1989, a Russian nuclear submarine called *Komsomolets* sank when a fire broke out inside it and the titanium hull fell apart. In 2000, another Russian submarine called *Kursk* sank in the Barents Sea. Investigators still do not know whether *Kursk* crashed into another submarine or exploded because of a faulty torpedo, but even its super-strong titanium double hull could not prevent the disaster.

*The layer of titanium in modern wetsuits makes them much warmer than their neoprene counterparts.*

# Periodic table

Everything in the universe is made from combinations of substances called elements. Elements consist of tiny atoms that are too small to see. Atoms are the building blocks of matter.

The character of an atom depends on how many even tinier particles (called protons) there are in its center, or nucleus. An element's atomic number is the same as the number of its protons.

Scientists have found around 110 different elements. About 90 elements occur naturally on Earth. The rest have been made in experiments.

All these elements are set out on a chart called the periodic table. This lists all the elements in order according to their atomic number.

The elements at the left of the table are metals. Those at the right are nonmetals. Between the metals and the nonmetals are the metalloids, which sometimes act like metals and sometimes like nonmetals.

- On the left of the table are the alkali metals. These elements have just one electron in their outer shells.
- On the right of the periodic table are the noble gases. These elements have full outer shells.
- Elements in the same group have the same number of electrons in their outer shells.
- Elements get more reactive as you go down a group.
- The number of electrons orbiting the nucleus increases down each group.
- The transition metals are in the middle of the table, between Groups II and III.

| Group I | Group II | Transition metals | | | | | | |
|---|---|---|---|---|---|---|---|---|
| 1 H Hydrogen 1 | | | | | | | | |
| 3 Li Lithium 7 | 4 Be Beryllium 9 | | | | | | | |
| 11 Na Sodium 23 | 12 Mg Magnesium 24 | | | | | | | |
| 19 K Potassium 39 | 20 Ca Calcium 40 | 21 Sc Scandium 45 | 22 Ti Titanium 48 | 23 V Vanadium 51 | 24 Cr Chromium 52 | 25 Mn Manganese 55 | 26 Fe Iron 56 | 27 Co Cobalt 59 |
| 37 Rb Rubidium 85 | 38 Sr Strontium 88 | 39 Y Yttrium 89 | 40 Zr Zirconium 91 | 41 Nb Niobium 93 | 42 Mo Molybdenum 96 | 43 Tc Technetium (98) | 44 Ru Ruthenium 101 | 45 Rh Rhodium 103 |
| 55 Cs Cesium 133 | 56 Ba Barium 137 | 71 Lu Lutetium 175 | 72 Hf Hafnium 179 | 73 Ta Tantalum 181 | 74 W Tungsten 184 | 75 Re Rhenium 186 | 76 Os Osmium 190 | 77 Ir Iridium 192 |
| 87 Fr Francium 223 | 88 Ra Radium 226 | 103 Lr Lawrencium (260) | 104 Unq Unnilquadium (261) | 105 Unp Unnilpentium (262) | 106 Unh Unnilhexium (263) | 107 Uns Unnilseptium (?) | 108 Uno Unniloctium (?) | 109 Une Unnilenium (?) |

| | | | | | |
|---|---|---|---|---|---|
| **Lanthanide elements** | 57 La Lanthanum 139 | 58 Ce Cerium 140 | 59 Pr Praseodymium 141 | 60 Nd Neodymium 144 | 61 Pm Promethium (145) |
| **Actinide elements** | 89 Ac Actinium 227 | 90 Th Thorium 232 | 91 Pa Protactinium 231 | 92 U Uranium 238 | 93 Np Neptunium (237) |

The horizontal rows are called periods. As you go across a period, the atomic number increases by one from each element to the next. The vertical columns are called groups. Elements get heavier as you go down a group. All the elements in a group have the same number of electrons in their outer shells. This means they react in similar ways.

The transition metals fall between Groups II and III. Their electron shells fill up in an unusual way. The lanthanide elements and the actinide elements are set apart from the main table to make it easier to read. All the lanthanide elements and the actinide elements are quite rare.

## Titanium in the table

Titanium's atomic number is 22, so it has 22 protons in its nucleus. This element is positioned in the middle of the periodic table in a group known as the transition elements. Titanium is the second most abundant transition element after iron. Like most other transition elements, titanium's compounds tend to be colored.

*Metals*

*Metalloids (semimetals)*

*Nonmetals*

| Key | |
|---|---|
| 22 | Atomic (proton) number |
| Ti | Symbol |
| Titanium | Name |
| 48 | Atomic mass |

| | | | Group III | Group IV | Group V | Group VI | Group VII | Group VIII |
|---|---|---|---|---|---|---|---|---|
| | | | | | | | | 2 He Helium 4 |
| | | | 5 B Boron 11 | 6 C Carbon 12 | 7 N Nitrogen 14 | 8 O Oxygen 16 | 9 F Fluorine 19 | 10 Ne Neon 20 |
| | | | 13 Al Aluminum 27 | 14 Si Silicon 28 | 15 P Phosphorus 31 | 16 S Sulfur 32 | 17 Cl Chlorine 35 | 18 Ar Argon 40 |
| 28 Ni Nickel 59 | 29 Cu Copper 64 | 30 Zn Zinc 65 | 31 Ga Gallium 70 | 32 Ge Germanium 73 | 33 As Arsenic 75 | 34 Se Selenium 79 | 35 Br Bromine 80 | 36 Kr Krypton 84 |
| 46 Pd Palladium 106 | 47 Ag Silver 108 | 48 Cd Cadmium 112 | 49 In Indium 115 | 50 Sn Tin 119 | 51 Sb Antimony 122 | 52 Te Tellurium 128 | 53 I Iodine 127 | 54 Xe Xenon 131 |
| 78 Pt Platinum 195 | 79 Au Gold 197 | 80 Hg Mercury 201 | 81 Tl Thallium 204 | 82 Pb Lead 207 | 83 Bi Bismuth 209 | 84 Po Polonium (209) | 85 At Astatine (210) | 86 Rn Radon (222) |

| | | | | | | | | |
|---|---|---|---|---|---|---|---|---|
| 62 Sm Samarium 150 | 63 Eu Europium 152 | 64 Gd Gadolinium 157 | 65 Tb Terbium 159 | 66 Dy Dysprosium 163 | 67 Ho Holmium 165 | 68 Er Erbium 167 | 69 Tm Thulium 169 | 70 Yb Ytterbium 173 |
| 94 Pu Plutonium (244) | 95 Am Americium (243) | 96 Cm Curium (247) | 97 Bk Berkelium (247) | 98 Cf Californium (251) | 99 Es Einsteinium (252) | 100 Fm Fermium (257) | 101 Md Mendelevium (258) | 102 No Nobelium (259) |

# Chemical reactions

Chemical reactions are going on around us all the time. Some reactions involve just two substances; others many more. But whenever a reaction takes place, at least one substance is changed.

In a chemical reaction, the atoms stay the same. But they join up in different combinations to form new molecules.

ATOMS AT WORK

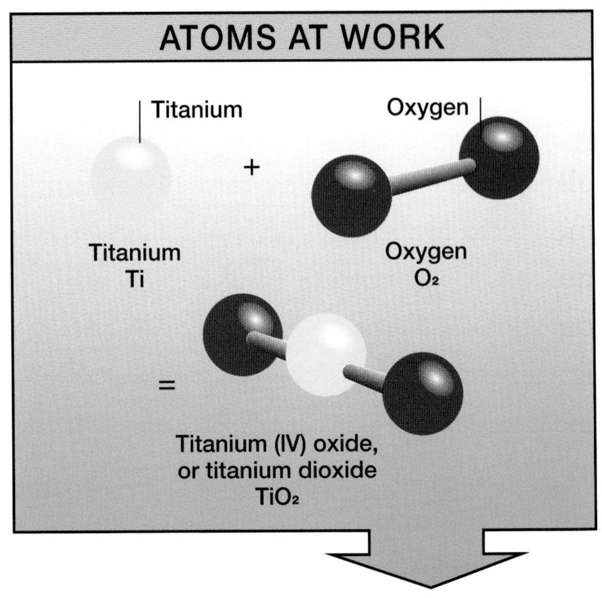


The reaction that takes place when titanium reacts with oxygen can be written like this:

$$Ti + O_2 \rightarrow TiO_2$$

*This is the equipment used in the Kroll process—a chemical reaction that separates titanium from its ores. The process was developed by German chemist William A. Kroll in 1937.*

## Writing an equation

Chemical reactions can be described by writing down the atoms and molecules before the reaction and the atoms and molecules after the reaction. The number of atoms before will be the same as the number of atoms after. Chemists write the reaction as an equation. This shows what happens in the chemical reaction.

## Making it balance

When the numbers of each atom on both sides of the equation are equal, the equation is balanced. If the numbers are not equal, something is wrong. A chemist adjusts the number of atoms involved until the equation does balance.

# Glossary

**alloy:** A mixture of a metal with one or more other elements.
**atom:** The smallest part of an element that has all the properties of that element. Each atom is less than a millionth of an inch in diameter.
**atomic mass:** The number of protons and neutrons in an atom.
**atomic number:** The number of protons in an atom.
**bond:** The attraction between two atoms, or ions, that holds them together.
**compound:** A substance made of two or more elements chemically joined together. Titanium dioxide is a compound made up of one titanium and two oxygen atoms.
**corrosion:** The eating away of a material by reaction with other chemicals, often oxygen and water vapor in the air.
**crystal:** A solid substance in which the atoms are arranged in a regular, three-dimensional pattern.
**electron:** A tiny particle with a negative charge. Electrons are found inside atoms, where they revolve around the nucleus in layers called electron shells.
**element:** A substance that is made from only one type of atom.
**ion:** An atom that has lost or gained electrons. Ions have either a positive or negative electrical charge.
**isotopes:** Atoms of an element with the same number of protons and electrons but different numbers of neutrons.
**Kroll process:** A chemical reaction, developed by German chemist William A. Kroll, to separate titanium from its ores.
**metal:** An element on the left-hand side of the periodic table.
**molecule:** A particle that contains atoms held together by chemical bonds.
**neutron:** A tiny particle with no electrical charge. It is found in the nucleus of every atom except hydrogen.
**nonmetal:** An element on the right-hand side of the periodic table.
**nucleus:** The dense center of an atom.
**ore:** A compound that contains a useful element, usually a metal, mixed together with other elements.
**periodic table:** A chart of all the chemical elements laid out in order of their atomic number.
**products:** The substances formed in a chemical reaction.
**proton:** A tiny particle with a positive charge. Protons are found inside the nucleus of an atom.
**reactants:** The substances that react together in a chemical reaction.
**transition metals:** The group of metals that form a block in the middle of the periodic table.
**valency:** The usual number of bonds an atom can form with other atoms.

# Index